MY FIRST ISLAMIC

COLORING BOOK

ISBN: 978-1-988779-13-3

Dépôt légal : bibliothèque et archives nationales du Québec, 2019.
Dépôt légal : bibliothèque et archives Canada, 2019.

Product Manager	: Bachar Karroum
Illustrator	: Jesus Vazquez Prada
Graphic Designer	: Samuel Gabriel
Cover Designer	: Rebecca Covers

In the name of God!

Before your child embarks on its coloring adventure, we suggest that you read through the book with him or her. This will help your child learn more about Islam and the prophet, and develop the desire to do good deeds.

Islam is based on five pillars:
Shahada, Salah, Zakat, Sawm and Hajj.

Zakat, the third pillar of Islam, is giving charity and helping the poor and the needy.

One of the greatest of deeds in Islam is showing kindness to the weak and the sick, taking care of them and looking after them.

Prophet Muhammad (PBUH) respected the aged and elderly. Follow his example, give a hand to the elderly, whenever they are in need.

Did you know that animal abuse is prohibited in Islam? Always treat them nicely. Help an injured animal when you can.

Prophet Muhammad (PBUH) always gave a hand to those in need of his help, and encouraged us to do the same.

Islam teaches us to be kind to our parents and respect them at all times.

The Prophet always helped with household chores, taking care of the home. Give a hand. Help your parents do the dishes.

Prophet Muhammad (PBUH) encouraged us to engage in good deeds, even smalls ones, such as smiling at one another. Sharing is caring, share a snack with a friend.

Praying (Salah) takes us away from making mistakes and committing sins. Did you know Prophet Muhammad (PBUH) never missed his prayers?

As Muslims, we must not rebuff the seeker. We should always help those in need or when asked a favor.

Protecting the environment is an important aspect of Islam.

Prophet Muhammad (PBUH) loved the Earth and encouraged us to plant more trees. Support our planet and plant a tree!

Being stewards of the Earth, it is the responsibility of Muslims to take care of the environment in a proactive manner.

Islam teaches us not to waste water, food or anything that Allah has blessed us with. We must use them carefully. Be mindful, don't waste too much water when you shower.

Did you know, during Ramadan, Muslims make it a point to recite more of the Quran in order to earn more rewards from Allah.

As Muslims, we must always remember to be kind to our parents.

The Prophet was especially considerate of orphans and asked his followers to take special care of them as they did not have parents to look after them.

Prophet Muhammad (PBUH) encouraged us to be kind to all animals, birds and insects.

The Prophet treated animals with kindness and taught us to do the same. If you have a pet, take good care of it.

Islam teaches us the importance of time, to using it wisely and keep on learning. Did you learn something new today?

We should remember to say Bismillah before, and Alhamdulillah after eating and drinking.

Islam teaches to be good to our relatives and maintain healthy relationships.

Friday is a holy day, the time of the week when Muslims go to the masjid and offer prayers in congregation.

Islam teaches us to be kind to our neighbor. Bake a cake or share some homemade food/dessert with your neighbor.

The Prophet always shared everything he had with the poor and taught us to be the same by treating them well and giving them charity.

The Prophet advised us to stay curious and increase our knowledge. Discover, go to the library and read a book.

Before the Eid al-Fitr prayer, Muslims give Zakat al-Fitr.
It is charity donated in the form of food or money which is then
distributed to the poor.

On the day of Eid, Muslims dress in their new or best clothes and attend a special Eid prayer at the Masjid.

After the Eid prayer, Muslims celebrate Eid together with family and friends by exchanging gifts and warm wishes.

Made in United States
North Haven, CT
14 April 2022

18265074R00037